What We Have in Common
A Brim Coloring Book

Written by Jane Landey

Edited by David Austin

Drawings by David Austin and Jane Austin

Published by CreateSpace : An Amazon Company.

Printed in U.S.A.

Introduction

What We Have in Common.

Brim Coloring Books enable children to color the drawings as they read along! The books display the similarities of related animals. In this series, the skunk and the squirrel are compared. The facts enable children to appreciate common values. Thus, imbibing in them interest towards animals which could make them appreciate what they have in common with one another.

THE SKUNK

AND

THE SQUIRREL

The Skunk and the Squirrel are animals that love to climb trees. The Skunk is bigger than the Squirrel. They are animals that fascinate people.

The Skunk and the Squirrel meet on a branch of a big tree.

I am a Skunk.

I am a Squirrel.

I can eat in bins, says the Skunk.

I pick fruits too, says the Squirrel.

I have a huge tail.

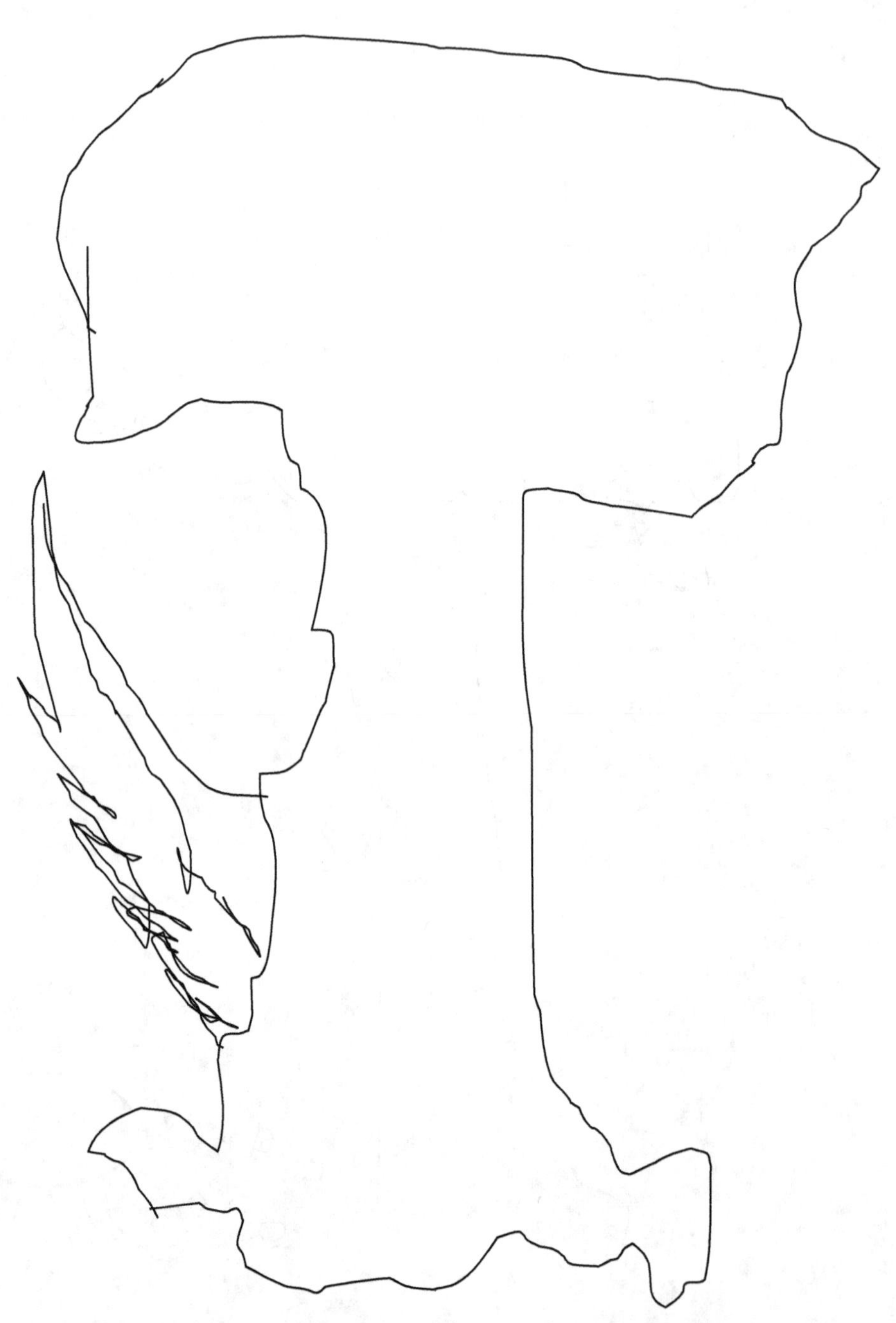

I have a huge tail too!

I can stand on my feet Mister Squirrel!

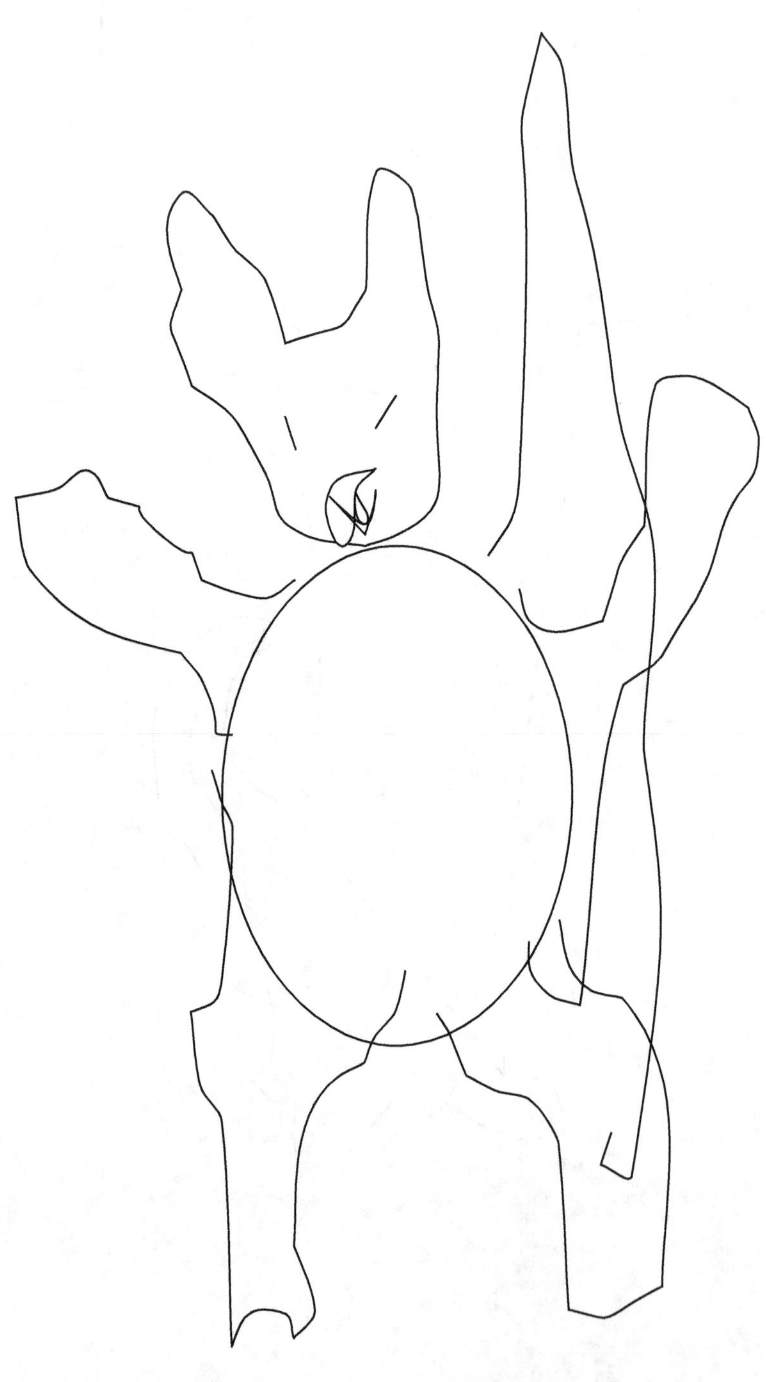

I can too Mister Skunk!

My ears are short!

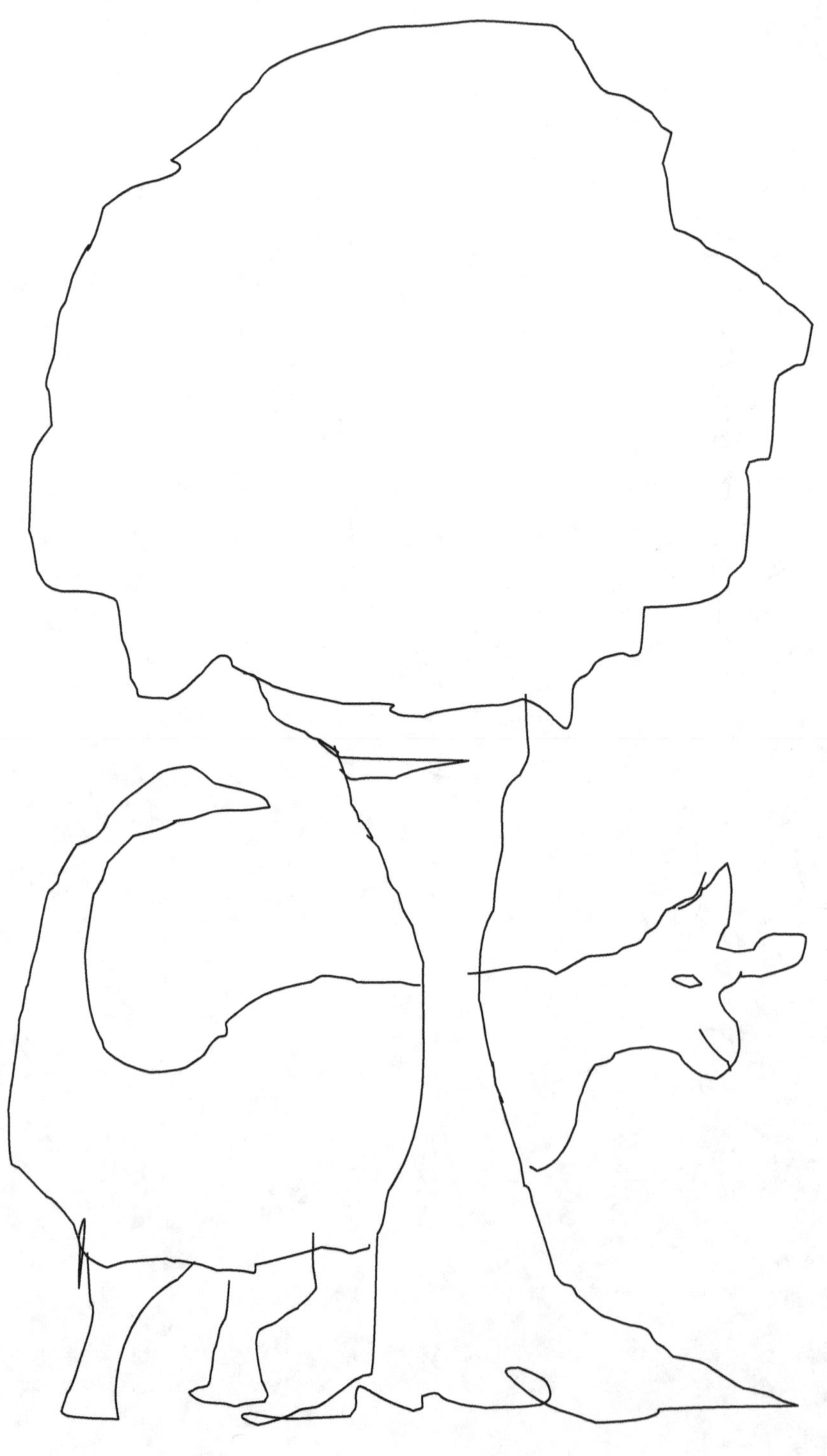

My ears are short and they stick out too!

If I am scared, I spray anyone that comes my way!

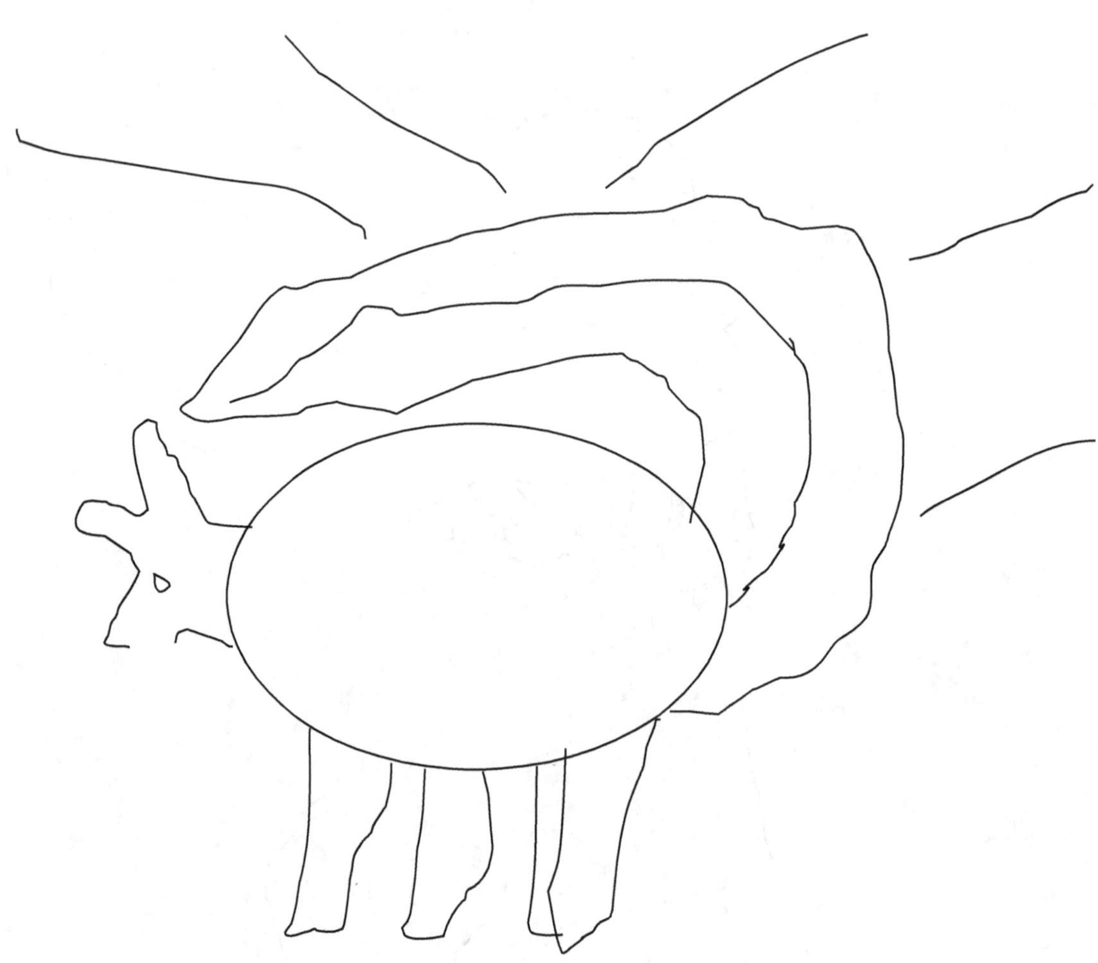

I wink at anyone that stares at me!

I can hide in trunks of trees!

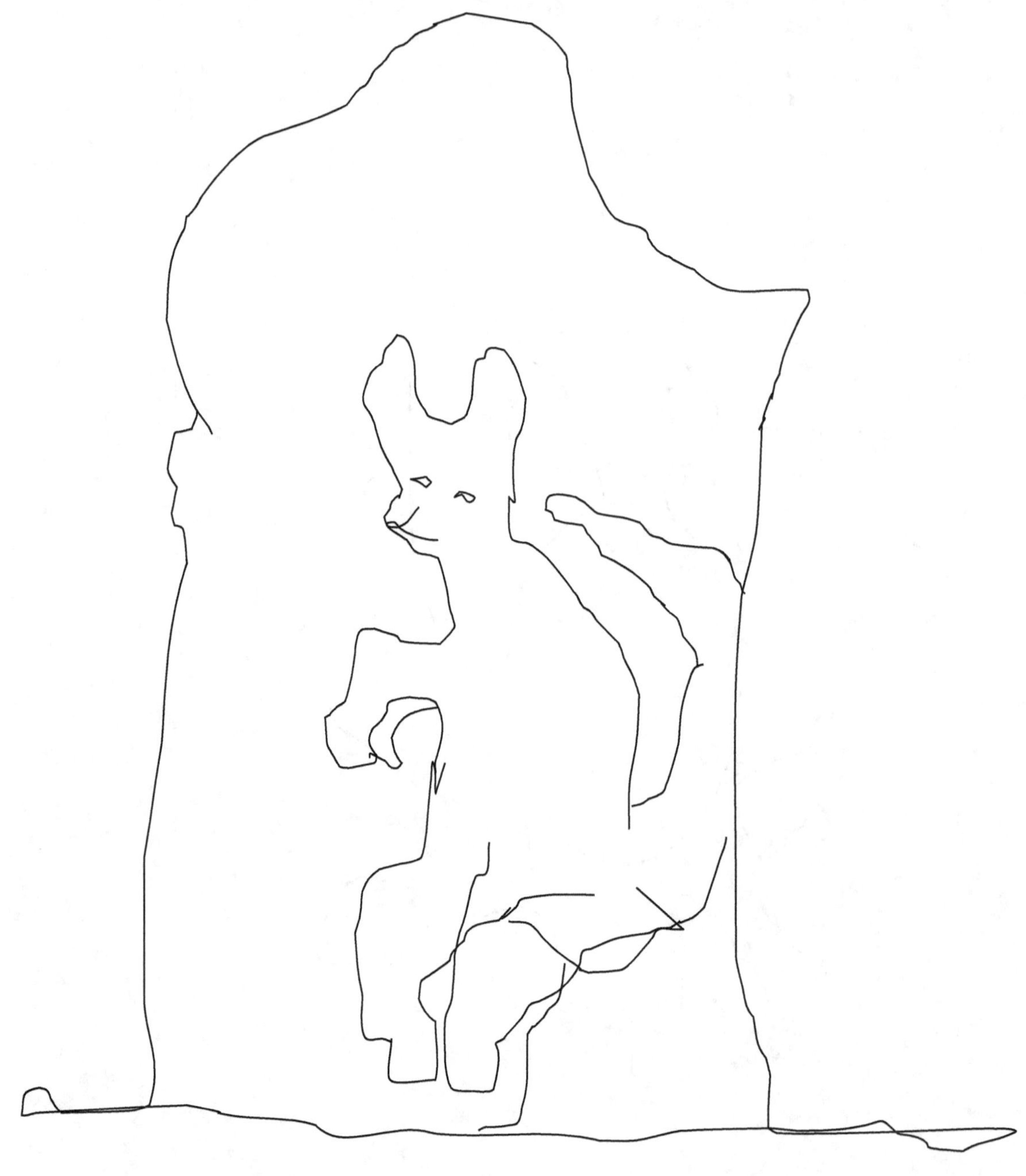

I play and hide in trunks of trees!

Do you want to see how I spray?

Of course yes but please don't spray
me!

Purrrrrhr!

Oh, it stinks!

I asked before I did it!

I didn't know it would be that smelly!

Do you want another spray?

No, no, no!

I would love to show you around.

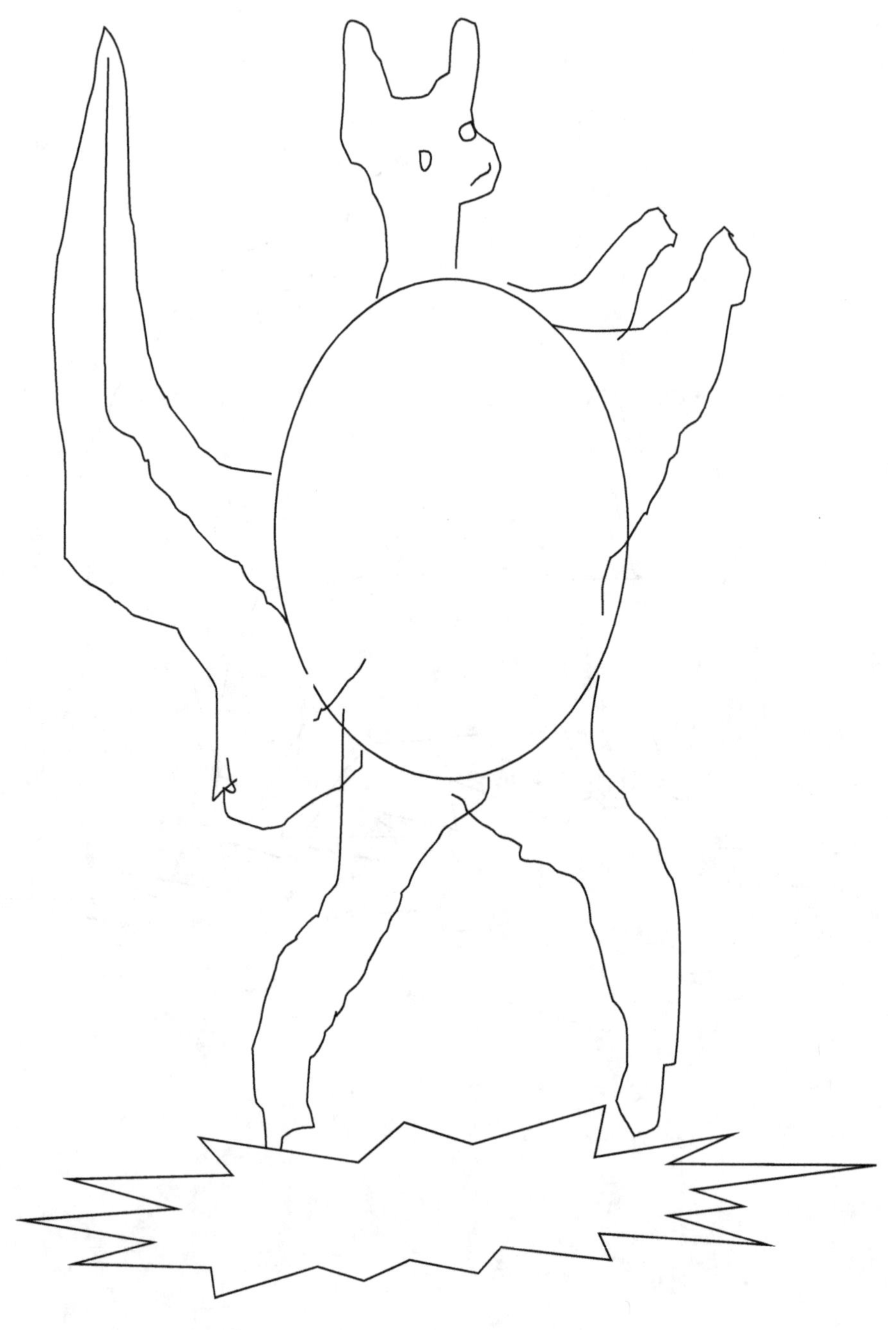

Not in this smelly place!

Do you know people are afraid of me because I can spray them?

Of course anyone would be!

How about you Mister Squirrel?

I am not afraid!

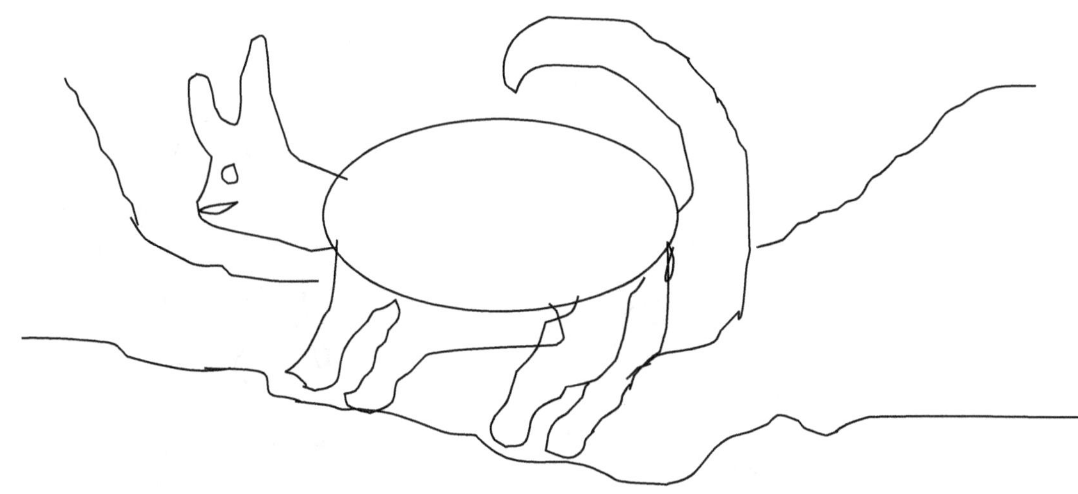

People love to play with you.

Yes! I play with them and I won't spray them!

Bye, see you some other time my new friend!

Bye, see you around!

What We Have in Common Brim Coloring Books

Crocodile and Alligator

Turtle and Tortoise

Starfish and Octopus

Worm and Snake

Vulture and Turkey

Ostrich and Emu

Weka and Kiwi

Bat and Rat

Camel and Llama

Duck and Pelican

Kangaroo and Wallaby

Pig and Tapir

Skunk and Squirrel

Hedge and Anteater

Cat and Owl

Elephant and Rhinoceros

Dog and Fox

Buffalo and Bull

Leopard and Cheetah

Horse and Zebra

www.ingramcontent.com/pod-product-compliance
Lightning Source LLC
Chambersburg PA
CBHW081255250726
48654CB00012B/1614